21 IRRESISTIBLE RECIPES FOR COUPLES

Joe Beam, Ph.D.

KeepTheFaith™
Contagious Encouragement!™

21 Irresistible Recipes For Couples

www.joebeam.com

Published by Keep the Faith Publishing, a Division of Big Oyo, LLC
2000 Mallory Lane, Suite 130-237
Franklin, Tennessee 37067
www.keepthefaith.com

Version KTF.001.2016.01

EDITIONS
Paperback: 9780996300520
E-Book: 9780996300537

Cover Design: Kim Russell | Wahoo Designs

Digital Design and Typeset: Telemachus Press, LLC
www.telemachuspress.com

International English Version

Joe Beam is featured on KeepTheFaith Radio

America's #1 faith-based syndicated radio show

To experience **Contagious Encouragement 24/7** visit

www.KeepTheFaith.com

Live radio, podcasts, events, articles, and first-person testimonies will help you discover the life-changing—and world-changing—faith to become the best you ever!

Table of Contents

Love is patient and kind. Love is not jealous or boastful or proud or rude. It does not demand its own way. It is not irritable, and it keeps no record of being wronged. It does not rejoice about injustice but rejoices whenever the truth wins out. Love never gives up, never loses faith, is always hopeful, and endures through every circumstance.

—1 Corinthians 13:4-7, NLT

Note To Reader:

You will love and grow from this short book if …

You and your spouse have a great marriage but both desire to grow even closer to one another;

You and your spouse are barely keeping your heads above water in marriage; if things don't change soon, your marriage isn't going to survive;

You have never been married and want to know what the key success factors for a "forever" marriage are;

You have been married and are still hurt from the divorce, but want to better understand where things went wrong so you can prepare for a new future with a loving marriage;

You have a friend who has a struggling marriage and you want to learn some key insights to offer help;

You are reading this book along with your spouse or are reading it alone because you are the only one committed to your marriage right now.

Wherever you are in your relationship right now, open your heart to the incredible grace of God to renew you, the one you love, and your marriage.

Chapter 1
The *Intimacy* Recipe

In my mind, marriage is a spiritual partnership and union in which we willingly give and receive love, create and share intimacy, and open ourselves to be available and accessible to another human being in order to heal, learn and grow.

—*Iyanla Vanzant*

IN NATIONAL SURVEYS men tend to define intimacy in terms of action. For example, ask a group of men how to explain intimacy and typically sex appears somewhere in the discussion. However, it isn't just sex that they consider to be intimacy. For a man it can be any kind of action he does with or for the woman he loves. If his wife were to say, "We need more intimacy," the husband might respond, "What do you mean? I built you a gazebo!"

Women tend to think differently about intimacy. When speaking in Texas a few years back, a woman from the audience described intimacy as the following: "If you just say the word intimacy slower, you'll have it: It's 'into me see.'" She was right. That's what true intimacy is—transparency, openness, and vulnerability.

When we were very young, we learned that we would be rejected by some people if we don't do what they want us to do, think what they want us to think, or feel what they want us to feel. To be accepted, we learned to pretend to be whatever it is the person we care about wants us to be. To do that, we build a metaphorical wall and hide our true selves behind it. Then we paint the picture on their side of the wall of what they wish us to be. The real "me" stays hidden behind that wall, afraid to let people see us as we really are. Why? Sometimes it's because we fear we will be rejected if we don't meet others' expectations. Other times we hide because we don't know what another person expects us to be; even though we don't know what they want, we fear that it isn't our genuine selves. We hide because we know we're flawed. We think, "If I'm flawed, you may not accept me."

I know I've struggled in the past with allowing others to see the true me because there are some days when I don't like myself. Days when I don't accept myself. That caused me to fear others would have trouble accepting me, too. I would paint their side of my wall with a picture of what I thought they wanted me to be. However, I knew they weren't seeing the real me. Therefore, when they said, "I like you," or "I love you," I didn't believe it because I figured they only liked what I painted, what I pretended to be, rather than my real self.

Finally, I came to realize that the only way to discern whether someone truly loved *me* was to take bricks off my wall and reveal my true self, to show others who I really am. That meant that rather than pretending to feel, think or act like what someone wanted me to be, I had to become transparent. Of course, that made me extremely vulnerable to being hurt. If someone rejected the person I pretended to be, I could rationalize, "Well, that's not who I really am anyway." If someone rejected the real me, there was no explaining it away. They saw me as I truly am and found me unacceptable.

That's why most of us hide our true selves behind walls and refuse to allow others a clear look back there.

Unfortunately, it's also why so few people experience true intimacy. Intimacy only occurs when two people allow themselves to be truly revealed to each other. I've long since forgotten the person in history who first phrased it this way, but **intimacy follows when two people can allow their souls to get naked with each other.**

If you want intimacy, you must allow your soul to go naked.

The only way to do that is to reveal your true self, if only a little at a time. To continue our illustration of the wall, you remove one of the bricks that hides the true you from view. You reveal something about yourself, which you fear may cause the other person to reject you. Doing that can be scary. If the person you love rejects the painting you pretend to be, you can pretend to be someone else. If they reject the person you really are, you have nothing else. You feel totally and completely rejected.

If my illustration of the wall makes sense to you, then you likely understand that when a person takes a brick off the wall, she doesn't throw it aside. She entrusts it to you. When she takes a brick off her wall so that you may learn something about her, which she wasn't sure you'd be willing to accept, it makes her vulnerable. Now you have the brick; you have something you can hurt her with. When she is confident that you will protect and cherish the brick she gave – you will not use that knowledge about her to hurt her – she'll hand you another one. She'll tell you something else about her that she fears you may not like.

Maybe she'll tell you about something she did that she wishes had never happened. Possibly she'll tell you about a desire she has that she feels she shouldn't. Perhaps she'll even share with you a dream she wishes to fulfill that she fears others would think crazy or impossible to accomplish.

If you continue to accept her, even though you may not agree with her, then she'll keep taking off more and more bricks in an effort to reveal the real person inside. And then when you say, "I love you," she believes it. Well, at least to a degree. If she's taken off a few bricks so that you see a little of the true her, she believes it a little. If she's taken off a lot and has become truly transparent, then she believes it a lot. As long as she knows she's hiding part of herself from you, she may have some doubts when you say you love her. She may well have this lingering thought that if you knew THAT OTHER THING about her, maybe you wouldn't love her.

How fast will a person remove bricks? Some people take off a brick every five minutes; some take one off every five months. It's based on their experiences of being loved or rejected in the past, their personalities, and the culture they grew up in.

Do people ever put bricks back on the wall?

Yes.

If at any point you take one of his bricks that he entrusted to you and then hurt him with it by throwing it back at him, he'll put another brick in its place. Maybe two or three higher and two or three thicker.

If you give the brick he entrusted to you to someone else, giving them a replica of his brick by telling them what he's told you, sharing his secrets, it will hurt him deeply. He will put bricks back on the wall. In fact, he can get so hurt that he might put bricks on higher and thicker than they were before. He can place those bricks so high and so thick to the point that he doesn't care what you think about him because he's walled you off completely.

How can a couple create intimacy? The two of you have to develop a relationship where each person can honestly say, “I know you're not perfect, but I can and do love you as you are. I will make it safe for you to take off every brick you are willing to share with me.” True intimacy occurs when each partner feels safe to take off the bricks, to reveal who each is, what each desires, and even what each fears.

You start off lightly, slowly, gently. You don't bulldoze down the wall because that’s much too dangerous. You take off a brick and observe how your partner handles it. It doesn't mean there won’t be hurt; there's occasional hurt in any relationship. However there is a great difference between being hurt by an inconsequential or foolish act or statement, and being hurt with one of your bricks. You shared that brick because you felt safe; it’s shattering to find out it’s not safe. If someone you love hurts you with the brick that you provided, that thing you made yourself vulnerable by sharing, it cuts a deep wound that is slow to heal … if it ever heals.

Intimacy is openness, transparency, vulnerability. Can intimacy lead to great sex and a great relationship in every other dimension? Absolutely. Acceptance that comes through intimacy is the key to a loving relationship.

One of my students at the Christian university where I teach human sexuality approached me after class. I could see that something was bothering her and that she really wanted to talk. After a few minutes of casual conversation, she told me, “I'm 22 and a senior in college. But when I was 16, I became involved in a sexual relationship, and now I'm worried that I can never, ever enjoy a relationship with another guy. I will always wonder if I should tell any new boyfriend about what happened to me. I mean, what if I told him and he rejected me?"

I encouraged her that, if she ever does intend to marry, she needs a man with whom she can share her past. She doesn't start by telling about a past sexual relationship, of course. She should start with lesser bricks, smaller bricks. As the relationship develops, she can observe whether he accepts her as she is, not only as he wishes her to be. When she is sure of that, she can tell him the things that scare her, the things that she's afraid he may reject her for, things that are threatening.

I emphasized that before she marries any man, she should be able to have a relationship in which she can tell him any story. He may likely regret that she's had the experience. He may offer sympathy: "I'm so sorry that happened to you," or "I wish that hadn't happened." I urged her to find a man who loves her and accepts her as she is, with whatever past she's lived, even if both of them wish it hadn't happened.

The 1st Recipe

If you want intimacy with another person, you have to take bricks from your wall and give them to that person. You must also give your partner the ability to take off bricks and give them to you. You won't always like what you hear;

sometimes it will hurt. If you can accept and love that person through the pain, he or she can take off more bricks and find more intimacy with you. You reciprocate. When you experience trust, you give trust as well. Start off with the bricks that are not so threatening, but eventually work down to the others. You, as a couple, can create an intimate relationship with deep, abiding, lifelong love.

Chapter 2
The *Bad Day* Recipe

For a marriage relationship to flourish, there must be intimacy. It takes an enormous amount of courage to say to your spouse, "This is me. I'm not proud of it—in fact, I'm a little embarrassed by it—but this is who I am."

—Bill Hybels

UNFORTUNATELY, IT APPEARS that we've come to believe that life is a 'happily ever after' business, similar to the fairy tales we heard as children. Nowhere can that belief be more problematic than in marriage. We get married thinking, "We're standing here in front of this clergyman, and we're making these vows to each other. Our family and friends are here, and it's going to be 'happily ever after.'"

Unfortunately, we tend to look at our wedding pictures thinking they represent everything that will happen from now on. The problem is that the wedding pictures are of a particular day and a particular event (and sometimes the weddings aren't even that great). When the flashbulbs stop, life tumbles in.

When we are falling in love we tend not to notice the flaws in the other person. We tend to think that he or she is just wonderful—Prince Charming or Cinderella. But if you think about it, even Prince Charming had problems. He went from Snow White to Cinderella and several other girls. Yes, I know he wasn't real, but even in fairy tales, just as in real life, no one is perfect.

Before marriage, you likely thought, "Every day is going to be marital bliss. It's going to wonderful. She'll be waiting for me when I walk through the door, and she'll shower me with kisses." Then, the day comes when you realize that your expectations didn't become reality. Marriage can be great most of the time, but definitely not all of the time. Life tumbles in. Spouses get sick; financial difficulties happen. When you have children you'll have a whole new set of experiences. Not only are you and your spouse flawed, your children are flawed, too.

Should you judge your marriage based on how you feel on any given day? Absolutely not. Feelings will go up and they will go down. Scholars and poets alike talk about commitment and intimacy and passion in marriage. Certainly those qualities are real; but even those realities fluctuate.

I know a couple who, like many young couples, were so much in love with each other that they couldn't wait to get married. They married, and life was going okay for a while except that the husband was an entertainer and he traveled quite a bit. Not long into their marriage, it became apparent that it was going to be difficult for him to be a husband and travel as much as he was traveling, leaving his wife at home. He decided that, for the sake of the marriage, he needed to be with his wife and not travel as much. He modified his career. Interestingly, in his mind, he began to hold her responsible for his career change, even though it was his decision. Their first child was born with severe handicaps. Intellectually, he understood that's one of those things that happen, but emotionally he blamed his child's handicap on his wife.

He perceived his wife as the cause of his no longer performing on the stage. He saw her as the one who produced this child who had life-altering challenges. He loved his child and loved his wife, but he resented her to the point that he emotionally pushed her away, had very little to do with her, and isolated her. That led to serious problems in their marriage. Enough that they finally had a harrowing wakeup call from a crisis concerning her need for affection being fulfilled by another man. They worked it out and have a good marriage today. This is what he says about it today, "I know that it wasn't her fault that I left my career or that we had a handicapped child. I had this expectation of marriage being this wonderful thing that was great every day and where everything was just what you wanted it to be, but that is just not the case. I now accept that marriage has its ups and downs. Life has its ups and downs, and through them all I love my wife with all my heart. I will never neglect her again."

The 2nd Recipe

True love stands by each others side on the good days and stands even closer on the bad days.
—*Unknown*

On the good days, it's easy to be in love because everything feels good, but what about the days that aren't 'happily ever after'? Do they mean that your marriage is bad? No, they mean that you're experiencing life. What do you do in the bad times or when the days aren't great? Rather than pushing each other away, those are the times when you reach out to each other. Pull closer together and face whatever it is that life is throwing at you. I hope you have more great times than bad times, but don't judge your marriage by how well it aligns to fairy tale promises.

Chapter 3
The *Magic* Recipe

A successful marriage requires falling in love
many times, always with the same person.
—Mignon McLaughlin

A YOUNG WIFE who had been married less than six months approached me. She said simply, "The magic's gone."

"What do you mean the magic's gone?" I asked.

She said, "You know, at the beginning when he came home, he was always excited to see me. We'd wind up cuddling and kissing, could hardly even eat dinner because we were so much into holding each other. We took long walks and had long conversations. Now, when he comes home and I try to hug him, he gives me a hug back, but I can tell it's just ritual. Then he wants to sit and watch the television for a while and unwind. No long walks or talks. Not hours of holding each other. So I'm thinking, the magic's gone. Our marriage is over. He doesn't love me anymore."

I suggested to her that love is something that you feel differently on different days.

Sometimes, love is commitment. "I'm here for you because I need to be, I'm supposed to be, or you need me." What feels like emotionless commitment is actually a real kind of love.

Sometimes, love is intimacy, "I feel so close to you right now. Let's talk and talk into the wee hours of the night." This kind of intimacy is real love.

Sometimes, love is passionate. "I'd like to talk to you, but what I really want to do is to love you in more intense and physical ways right now." Passion is not only sex, but also missing each other, enjoying shared experiences, and thinking longingly about the other person. This kind of passion is real love.

These varying emotions you feel don't mean anything has changed about the magic. The magic of marriage is not about the intensity or the emotions you feel when you're a newlywed. The magic of marriage is the ability to be married fifty or sixty years or more. It's a deeper kind of thing. Is it always intense? Not in the same sense, no; but it's deeper and more abiding. It's an emotion that leads you to feel peace. It provides a feeling of security. It creates within you the feeling, "This is the person I know is there for me, no matter what, who cares for me on the good days, the bad days, and the indifferent days."

If you intend to judge your marriage based on whether you feel like its magical today, maybe you need to redefine marital *magic*. Marital magic is longevity. Marital magic is making it for the long haul. Marital magic is knowing that this person is with you for a lifetime.

Love doesn't always feel good. Sometimes love leads to actions a person doesn't want to do, but you do them because the beloved is in need. In short, love isn't about what you feel at a given moment. The greatest example of love ever given was by a man who didn't want to do it. It was a man who begged in a garden for God to take from Him the cup of suffering that awaited Him on a cross. Yet, He surrendered His will to the Father's. Isn't that an amazing act of love? Maybe we wouldn't call it magical because the word *magic* is not used in that respect in the Bible, but it was a love that was intense. A love that didn't rely on emotions at a given moment. If you're together and committed, if you do for each other what each needs, then that's the love of Christ. That's true love, even if it doesn't feel magical.

The 3rd Recipe

Recognize all the different kinds of love and commitment. Enjoy the days when you feel that intense ecstasy and passion. Those days can revive and renew. They can inspire us when we feel trapped in routine and disappointment. We need to know that we’re capable and that those times will come again. But, in the meantime, enjoy it when you can simply sit beside each other on the sofa, hold hands, and not say a word. Or he's watching TV or reading his book, you're writing out the week’s menu and making a grocery list, and everything is wonderful because you both know each of you is there. And then on the days when your love and commitment cost you more than you ever imagined, cling to those days, too. Love endures. It doesn’t give up.

Chapter 4
The *Investment* Recipe

The more you invest in a marriage, the more valuable it becomes.
—*Amy Grant*

MIKE JOHNSON AT Penn State University describes commitment as doing whatever it takes to keep a relationship alive. The level of investment parallels the level of commitment. He says that one thing that leads to strong commitment is a thing called irretrievable investment. What that means is that I put things into our relationship that I cannot get back. In other words, it's not tit-for-tat. It's not that I'm doing this because I get X in return. Instead, commitment means the more I do for you, the more I'm committed to you. I've given you so much of my life, so much of who and what I am that I can't give up on this investment.

One way to illustrate the investment/commitment connection is with a teenage boy and his first car. If he only uses it for transportation and doesn't care much about the car, likely he doesn’t care much for it. When he trades it for another car, he doesn't miss it at all. By contrast, consider the teenage boy that washes his car, waxes it, and works under the hood. He spends his free time making that car its best. The more that he works on it, the more he loves that car. As a matter of fact, when he's 50 years old, he may still have that same car in the garage somewhere because he has put so much into it.

If investment fosters commitment to a car, imagine how much more commitment it can bring to a relationship! When we start dating, we really reach out to and fulfill the other person. We rack our brains to find answers to questions like “How can I make him happy? What can I do today that will be good for her? Should I bring her flowers? Can I call during the middle of the day just to tell him how much I love him?”

The more of those things you do and the more of your energy and life you put into the other person, the more you find yourself loving that person because you’re giving that person your heart, interest, and passion.

Yes, the investment can make you more committed, but it also makes you love more.

An investment in your spouse benefits your emotions and also benefits your spouse. He knows there's somebody who loves him more than anything and who is more focused on him than on any other person or thing.

A few years ago a woman came to me and said, “I'm going to leave him. He wants too much attention—particularly in the bedroom. The problem is he doesn’t pay that much attention to me. I want to tell him, 'When you become a nicer guy, I'll do that for you.'”

I replied, “Obviously, it's your choice, but I've got a suggestion for you.”

“What’s that?” she asked.

“Do what he wants. He's not asking you to do anything sinful or bad, he's just wanting you to give him a lot more attention in that particular area of your life. Why don't you go buy some nice lingerie? Why don't you become more romantic? Why don't you try the candles and the bubble baths, and give him what he wants?”

She sighed and then responded, “But if I focus on him like that, I won't be getting anything in return.”

I explained, “I believe you will. Within a year, you'll find that he'll be the most attentive man in your life because you're giving him so much. I predict this will be an investment, which will yield lavish returns.”

She considered what I said before asking, “What if he doesn't?”

"Then when you leave him, it'll kill him. However, if your investment works, and I think it will, he'll love you more than he ever has. Besides, you might find that you forget who is giving and who is receiving."

About a year later, I saw her and asked if she had gotten the divorce like she originally thought she wanted.

Her jaw dropped as though I had asked her something absurd. "How can I divorce that man? He's the most wonderful man in the world! He shows me he loves me, he helps me around the house, he calls me during the day, he takes me on dates, and our bedroom life has become indescribably good! I love him!"

The 4th Recipe

Invest in your marriage. Invest in your spouse. If you want to have more commitment that can help you through the bad times when they come, do more for your spouse today. Do everything you can: Listen, talk, give gifts, and spend time. Those actions will increase your commitment and love for him or her. At the same time, because your spouse will appreciate that kind of attention, that kind of focus, and because he or she will feel so loved, it will increase his or her commitment and love towards you, as well.

Chapter 5

The *Self-Love* Recipe

If you can learn to love yourself and all the flaws, you can love other people so much better. And that makes you so happy.
—*Kristin Chenoweth*

I WAS HOSTING a call-in radio program when a woman phoned to explain why she didn't think she could stay with her husband anymore. Naturally, I asked her why.

"Well he's just too good to me," she said.

"What do you mean?" I asked.

She related all the things that he would do for her—things as small as opening the door for her and bringing her gifts even when it wasn't a special occasion.

The more I listened the more interested I became. My experience with thousands of marriages through my work at Marriage Helper was that people typically want out of relationships because those things *don't* happen, not because they do. But the more this woman's husband demonstrated the depth of his love, the more she wanted out of the relationship.

After listening to her for three or four minutes I interrupted her.

"May I ask you a question?"

"What's that?" she asked grudgingly.

"You don't really feel like you deserve any of these things, do you?"

"No, I don't," she responded with some defiance.

"So, it's not so much the fact that he's doing these nice things for you. It's that you don't feel you're worth them. Is that correct?"

"Yes," she finally said. "I don't feel worthy."

I gently pointed out to her that Jesus said that we are to love our neighbor as we love ourselves. A key to understanding that teaching is to understand that when we don't love ourselves, we have a difficult time loving others. It sounded to me as if she didn't love herself.

I asked, "Do you love yourself?"

She stumbled around for a couple of minutes trying to answer the question and finally said, “I don’t know.”

I said, “It may be impossible for you to love your husband until you learn to love yourself. I don’t mean in some vain, egotistical way, but with a healthy self-love that provides the foundation for loving others.”

There are many reasons people don't love themselves. Sometimes it's because of things they have done in the past. Sometimes it's because they grew up in a home where they were never taught anything about true love. They experienced rejection, criticism, and harshness, which resulted in never learning to love themselves. Sometimes it's because of things that were done to them, which they are now ashamed of, but at the time couldn’t control.

People who have difficulty loving others change only when they learn how to love themselves. Until they do, they tend to function in a push-pull relationship.

Someone in a push-pull relationship might think like this: “I really don't believe you can love me because I'm not worthy of being loved. I'll push you away, but in pushing you away, I'm hoping you're going to resist my pushing and instead pull me to you, demonstrating how much you love me anyway.”

The woman who called was an extreme case. Usually the push-pull continues until finally the partner being pushed has had enough. He thinks to himself, “You push me away repeatedly. You want me to demonstrate love, yet you punish me when I do. How can I ever make you happy?" Often, that's the spouse who wants out of the marriage because he or she feels they can't please the other and is emotionally exhausted. In her case, she was the one who wanted out. He kept trying to pull her to him emotionally, but she rejected his actions because she didn't feel worthy.

If you feel as this woman did, mark it down, you can come to understand and believe that you are worthwhile and that you are loveable. Your being loveable is not based on what you've done in your past. It's not based on what has been done to you.

So what is being loveable based on? What makes YOU a person worthy of being loved? Look into your heart. Don't look for perfection. You aren't. Do not look for confirmation that you're imperfect. You are. Don't look for the things you've done wrong or the wrong that has been done to you. Instead, look to see the true heart within you.

Do you care about people? Do you want to love? Do you want to be loved? Those show evidence of a heart that is good—not perfect-because we're all flawed—and a heart that is genuine and worth being loved.

Maybe I can simplify this with one question. Does God love you? The answer is yes, even if sometimes you wonder. Does He love you because you are perfect? No. "But God showed his great love for us by sending Christ to die for us while we were still sinners." (Romans 5:8) God can see you behind the wall where you're hiding. He knows how flawed you are—including the things you've done that you wish you hadn't—but loves you with an infinite love.

If you think about it, everyone is flawed—everyone you've ever met or known. Accept the fact that you are flawed also. Can you accept the fact that you are who you are? Can you accept the fact that you've done what you've done or you've had done to you what's been done? When you finally can, everything will change. The philosopher/psychologist Carl Rogers said, "When I accept myself as I am, I change." The way to love you is to accept you as you are.

Here's a project I want you to do. Sit down one day, and rather than thinking about all the things that make you feel that you're not lovely or lovable, write down the things that make you lovely and lovable. Come up with anything you possibly can. If you're willing to believe other people, ask them to tell you the same, not in a narcissistic, selfish, or arrogant sort of way, but to say, "I'm having trouble loving me, can you tell me what's lovely and lovable about me?" When they tell you, pay attention, hear what they say, and when you can accept that, you will begin to love you. When you finally love yourself as God wants you to do, you'll find that you can truly love another. Remember the great key that Jesus revealed when he said, "Love your neighbor as yourself."

Several years ago, I referred a couple to a counselor friend of mine. During one session, the wife confided to the counselor that she had been sexually abused as a child. The abuse led her to believe that she was dirty and not worthy of being loved. As a result, she had difficulty loving her husband. The counselor led her to understand that the abuse, terrible as it was, did not change her worth.

With her counselor's help, she told her husband about her childhood terror. He held her and shared her pain. Then he apologized for all the times he had pressured her sexually when she didn't want to be sexual. "If only I'd known the pain that you felt, I wouldn't have done that." Then the husband set about making it his business every day to help her understand that she was lovely and lovable—just as she was, without having to meet any criteria, standard, or anything else. From that day on, she learned how to accept her past, and she learned how to love him. They have built a tremendous marriage.

The 5th Recipe

In order for a marriage relationship to be healthy, each spouse needs to be emotionally healthy. For that to occur, each one needs to accept himself or herself, the past, and the present. Decide that you are worthwhile. You don't have to be perfect to be loved. God loves you just as you are. When you accept yourself and your past, no matter how bad or how good, you can love yourself. From that wholeness, the love and vulnerability of marriage can thrive. In the absence of that wholeness, the relationship will be plagued by misunderstandings and unrewarded attempts to compensate for the forces that threaten the relationship.

Chapter 6
The *Let's Talk* Recipe

Ultimately the bond of all companionship,
whether in marriage or in friendship, is
conversation.
—*Oscar Wilde*

I READ A study in which several men were asked, "How much time in an average week do you talk to your wife about something other than business?" (Business or procedural communication includes paying the bills, fixing up the house, disciplining the children, and so on.) The husbands estimated two hours of conversation per week. This study ignored procedural talk and tallied just the non-business conversational moments between husbands and wives. The guys who had estimated two hours of such communication were asked to wear voice-activated recorders. Researchers analyzed the data from the recorders. They found that the average length of time that these husbands were talking to their wives about non-business matters was fifteen minutes a week.

Sometimes couples think they are connecting with each other, but rather than truly connecting to each other, they're only dealing with the 'business' part of marriage and family.

How can you get past just business and truly talk with and understand your spouse?

The first thing you may have to do is find time to talk. In this hectic world, that means you have to make it part of your schedule. The television is off. The cell phones are put away. The kids are in bed, or at least not going to be intrusive. There's nothing that's going to interrupt conversation. At the beginning, if you're one of the couples who has been surviving on fifteen minutes per week and not used to uninterrupted, meaningful conversation, maybe you only set aside fifteen minutes a day.

Maybe you're thinking, "What do we talk about? If we're not talking about the children, the bills, or about repairing the house, what do we talk about?"

Here's the recipe that I believe works for all couples: Tell your stories.

Start with childhood stories. Take turns sharing and listening. Go back as far as you can remember and tell your husband or your wife, "This is something that happened to me when I was seven." The narratives don't have to be profound; they just have to tell your story.

Sharing our life events has profound merit. In life we are not the sum of our experiences. We are the sum of our interpretation of our experiences. That explains why two kids who grew up in the same home experiencing most of the same things come out with very different views of childhood.

The key here is not only to tell a story, but to allow yourself to relive it as you do. See it in your mind. Notice the details around you in the story. Allow yourself to experience your senses such as smell, touch, or taste. For example, if the story takes place in your grandmother's kitchen, allow your memory to smell the pie baking, the taste of it, the feel of its texture in your mouth.

Why?

Because reliving it does three things.

First, it brings back the emotions connected with the story.

Second, from the story, including the emotions, you may learn something about yourself that you've not allowed yourself to understand before now.

Third, as you learn more about how the story shaped you into who you are now, your spouse will also gain insight that he or she may not have previously had.

A couple I helped was having difficulty because of different ideas about spending choices. He always wanted to buy the best of everything. Whatever it was, he wanted the top brand, the most expensive. She was more frugal. She was constantly saying to him, "Why don't you buy something that is just as good, but not top of the line. We could save hundreds and sometimes thousands of dollars?" They were struggling to find common ground on spending until they took my advice and told stories from childhood.

This is the story he told her. "I remember when I was about to go back to school when I was entering the seventh grade. My parents had lived through the depression and were very frugal. So frugal that I had to wear hand-me-downs to school, or clothes we bought that were the cheapest they could find. All through the first six grades I had endured endless taunts, insults, and humiliation as the other kids made fun of what I wore. It was time to get my school clothes for the beginning of the school year. We were having dinner. I looked at my mother and father and said, 'School's about to start. We're going to get my clothes tomorrow. This year can we just get something that's decent? Every year all the kids make fun of me. I'm called the little poor boy. I'm tired of being humiliated. This year … this year … just this once, can we buy something good for me to wear so I can fit in with the other kids?"

"My parents replied as they always did, 'We lived through the depression. It may come again. We put all our money into these insured accounts. We have to save every penny and be as frugal as we can. You'll wear what we buy for you, and you'll like it. When the next depression comes, you'll be the one all the other kids envy.'"

As he spoke, he allowed himself to relive that situation in his mind. He started feeling the same emotions again. He began to weep because he was a humiliated little boy again. As he relived his story, in a very real way his wife entered his childhood.

A couple of things happened when he told that story. First, he had an epiphany. He suddenly realized, "My goodness! That's why I always want the best of everything. I don't want to be that poor little kid that gets made fun of again. I think that if I have nicer things I'll have more respect."

Even before he said those words, his wife had her 'aha' moment. She realized that's why he was driven to buy top brands. It dramatically changed her view of his spending.

Not only did the husband and wife begin to understand his desire to purchase only the best, but two things changed. First, she said, "You buy whatever you want, Babe. It's fine with me. I understand how important this is to you." Second, because he had had that revelatory experience by telling her the story and reliving it, he no longer had the compelling desire to buy the top of the line. He could buy things that were less expensive, but just as good. Their finances began to change. They weren't poor to begin with. His buying the best wasn't putting them in financial distress, but agreeing on spending choices made them both happier.

Not every story that's shared will be life-changing, but imagine having conversations where the two of you just sit and talk. He tells stories; she tells stories. These may be events you have related before, but this time you allow yourself to relive them. You can go through all of your life, telling story after story and eventually you'll come to telling stories of what happened last week, or yesterday, or even today at work. If you really want to know each other, understand the stories.

The 6th Recipe

Your interpretation of your experiences profoundly impacts who you are today. Go back to those experiences, relive them as you share your stories with your husband or wife, and you will both gain a better understanding of yourself and each other. Telling your stories creates more intimacy and transparency, revolutionizing the depth of your relationship.

Chapter 7
The *Listening* Recipe

One of the most sincere forms of respect is
actually listening to what another has to say.
—*Bryant McGill*

IN THE LAST chapter, I shared the success couples have had when they talk to each other for fifteen minutes every day. But sometimes, telling stories does not work because one person won't hear what the other person really is saying. Such was the case with this couple.

The couples who participate in our Marriage Helper 911 Workshop, an intense weekend for marriages in crisis, are encouraged to complete homework assignments. One couple was having great difficulty with assignments, which required them to write their answers, take turns reading them to each other, and then repeating back what the other person had said. The goal was to explore their ability to communicate with and understand each other. This couple simply couldn't do it. They wound up in an argument every time.

We connected them to a mentor couple who invited them into their home. The mentor couple observed that the husband would read his answer, and the wife would react to her interpretation of his answer, rather than to what he actually said. The mentor couple would then intervene gently and kindly, "I don't think you heard him. What he really said was …" The mentors would repeat what the husband had said and clarify as much as needed for the wife to grasp what he had said. She would then respond appropriately. Then, she would read her written answer, and he would interact inappropriately because he wasn't truly hearing what she said. Again, the mentor couple would intervene.

The couples met weekly for about a month until finally the formerly troubled couple was interacting in a healthy, transparent way. They were understanding and communicating because they were not listening for what they wanted (or expected) to hear. They were listening to hear what the other person was saying. They finally reached a point when if they did interrupt the other, the interruption was not to argue nor was it to correct or defend. It was simply to ask a clarifying question. "Are you saying this or are you saying that?"

They had learned to communicate. They were listening to hear the message coming from the heart of the other person, rather than reacting to a particular word, phrase, or intonation. During a later session, the mentor couple eyed one another, realized the other couple wasn't depending on them anymore, and quietly slipped away to their den where they watched television for the next hour until the other couple realized they were gone.

Once you have learned to listen, there's a second part: Consider what's behind the communication. Sometimes, when a person asks you a question, you want to consider, "What is really being asked here?" I can give an example from my marriage.

My wife, Alice, and I had been married for a short time and out of the blue one day Alice said, "If anything happened to me, would you get married again?"

I said, "No."

I found that "No" was the wrong answer. It upset her.

I knew since "No" was the wrong answer, the next time she asked that question I'd have the right answer.

A few months later, she asked the same question, "Would you get married again if anything happened to me?"

I said, "Yes."

That's when I discovered "Yes" was the wrong answer as well. She reacted just as badly to that answer as she had to the first one.

At that point, it dawned on me. “I’m not answering the right question.”

After a few more months, she asked the question again, “If anything happened to me, would you get married again?”

I gave a very honest answer, but now I was answering the question that she was really asking. I said, “I have no idea what I would do. I love you so much that I can’t think of life without you. I can't even contemplate what I would do. I want you to live as long as you possibly can because I love you, and I never want to even think about a day without you.”

That was the right answer. That was the answer to “the question behind the question.”

I suggest that before you answer some questions—or if you find yourself perplexed by your spouse’s reaction when you answer a question—to stop and ask yourself, “Was that really the question or is there another question behind the question.” If you realize there is one, answer that question instead.

Isn’t that hard work? Maybe. But what it comes down to is *listening hard* out of love and respect.

The 7th Recipe

Listen to your spouse’s heart. Listen to the true message he or she is communicating rather than the one you expect … or that you fear. Don't react to anything other than what your spouse truly is trying to communicate. Dig through all the questions, phrases, words, looks, and sighs; and filter out what's really being said. Inevitably somebody will choose a wrong word, or phrase a thought the wrong way. Do your best to respond to the heart of the question and interact with that. If couples really want to listen, they will ask clarifying questions. “Are you saying this? Help me understand that.” Focus on what your spouse is trying to communicate, rather than picking at the exact wording.

Listen for the heart; that’s when communication begins to enrich a relationship.

Chapter 8

The *Affirmation* Recipe

People will forget what you said, people will forget what you did, but people will never forget how you made them feel.

—Maya Angelou

WHEN ALICE AND I were newlyweds, we had gone to one of my speaking engagements and were driving back home through Birmingham, Alabama. We passed the Jaguar dealership. I looked over and saw those Jaguars sitting on the lot and said, "I want to buy a Jaguar."

Undoubtedly, the first thing that popped into my wife's mind was the negative balance in our checking account. Back then I was a minister at a very small church, which provided us with a very small salary. She surely must have been thinking, "You're a complete idiot. There is no way on earth you can buy a Jaguar."

Instead, this is what she said: “We both know that we can't afford one right now, but I know you. I know that you can do anything in life you choose to do. And if you want a Jaguar, you're the kind of man that someday will have one because you'll make things happen so that we can afford it. I believe you can do anything.”

Though she was thinking, “We have no money,” she affirmed me. She didn't affirm my idea; she couldn't suggest that it was a good time to buy a Jaguar right then. I could have never qualified for the loan, and attempting such a purchase would have caused us a great deal of trouble. However, she could still affirm me, and her affirmation made me believe in myself.

I remember hearing a minister of a large church talk about messages of confidence that spouses communicate to each other. He related the story of a guy at his church who was assigned to direct traffic in the parking lot as hundreds of members arrived and departed between service times. When the man’s wife heard about his new assignment, she said to him, “You know you can't do that. You're not organized. You'll get confused. You'll send people in the wrong direction. It will be a mess out there if you start directing traffic.”

The man instantly reacted to his wife’s harsh words. “You never think I can do anything. You never believe in me. I’m through listening to your criticism.”

Now, contrast those two stories. What do you think happened to the relationship in which she was telling him what he couldn't do, as opposed to the relationship Alice and I had when she told me, “You can't accomplish that dream right now, but I know you will”?

Which husband do you think felt better about his wife and marriage?

You can see the power of your affirmation even in children. How long does it take you to get a child to draw a second picture if you approve of the first picture? A child brings you a picture, you say something nice. In just a matter of minutes, there’s another picture. You exclaim, “Wow! That's the best picture of a horse I've ever seen.” To which she replies, “No Daddy, that's you.” Without hesitation, you chime, “And that's the best picture of me that I have ever seen.” She brings another and another and another. That's how powerful affirmation is. She likes getting it, and will continue to do things to make that happen.

On the other hand, the put-down has a different effect altogether. I recall speaking with one of the most successful men I have ever known. At that time, he was in his 70s. I asked this accomplished man, “What's your most vivid memory in life?” I expected that he would tell me about some famous person he met or some great accomplishment.

He said, “I was twelve years old. I spent half a day building a model airplane. I took it in to show my father. He looked at it and said, ‘Is that the best you can do?’ I went back into my room, crushed it into little pieces, threw it in the trash can, and never tried to make another model of anything in my life."

This response was from a man in his 70s who had accomplished amazing things, but his most vivid memory was his father's message of condemnation. A message of "You can't do that; you are not competent; you are not able" coming from someone we love and respect has a lasting impact.

What does this mean to your marriage? It means that sometimes you will disagree with each other. You'll have different desires. You'll want to go in different directions. Nevertheless, criticism of your spouse is not allowed. Even when you cannot go along with what your spouse wants, never put him or her down. Never make your spouse feel badly about himself or herself. Find the strength to give affirmation.

You give affirmation when you communicate "you did that well." Everybody loves the pat on the back. When dreams and plans go badly, you can still find words of encouragement: "I know that didn't work well, but I believe in you. I know who you are."

After many years of marriage, my wife Alice and I wound up divorced because I went off on a tangent in my life. Three years later, I asked her if she would take me back. All of her friends told her, "No. Never take him back. You can never trust him again." She rejected her friends' messages of condemnation. We remarried each other in 1987, and we are happy and very much in love with each other to this day. Her affirmation of me was the key.

Not long ago I heard somebody ask her, "Why would you do that? Why would you take him back?" That was a fair question, which deserved an honest answer. She said, "Because even though I knew that Joe had done such a bad thing, I believed that in his heart he was a good man. I recognized that the 'very good man' could take over, and Joe could again be the man he was. I believed in Joe."

That's why she married me again. You can imagine how that affirmation has impacted me. If any temptation comes through my life—any temptation at all that would cause me to hurt my wife or do something that would cause her pain—I think, "She really believes in me. I've got to live up to that belief." Affirmations from the ones closest to us have life-changing power.

The message of affirmation is rooted in the Bible. Consider how God views us. We disappoint him. We break His heart. Yet, He still affirms His work in us. Jesus affirmed a young man who was extremely impulsive and had a tendency to screw things up. Jesus said to hot-headed Peter, "I'm going to name you Rock." Isn't that an amazing thing? What Jesus saw in this man was what was going to be developed. Simon Peter would become a rock, a rock in the kingdom, a rock that was very powerful and used by God to accomplish His will on earth.

The 8th Recipe

Find the positive to affirm in your spouse. The things you affirm are the things that will be repeated. While you can't change another person, you certainly can help another person become better by affirming the choices, attitudes, and actions that are good.

Chapter 9
The *Power Words* Recipe

Words are singularly the most powerful force available to humanity. We can choose to use this force constructively with words of encouragement, or destructively using words of despair. Words have energy and power with the ability to help, to heal, to hinder, to hurt, to harm, to humiliate and to humble.

—*Yehuda Berg*

SOMETIMES WE TALK without thinking. Yet every time we say a word, that word has power because words always represent something. They represent ideas and concepts; they communicate what's in our heart. They reveal what we feel and what we think. Perhaps some words are just thrown away and have no meaning that has been thought through. But, even then, the other person is hearing something.

When we examine the research about why people divorce, we find that people typically divorce for one of three reasons: They don't feel loved, they don't feel liked, or they don't feel respected. Of course, it could be a combination of the three.

John Gottman has written about "divorce predictors." He calls them "The Four Horsemen of the Apocalypse." These predictors include criticism (attacking with the idea "what is wrong with you?"), contempt (disdain and condescension), defensiveness (self-justifying, self-protecting counter attack), and stonewalling (evading, obstructing, avoiding). Using any of the horsemen makes relationships worse. Removing the horsemen makes relationship better. For example, criticism of a spouse increases the likelihood of divorce. If one ceases being critical, it increases the likelihood of sustaining a marriage.

One couple that came to our Marriage Helper 911 Workshop for marriages in crisis vividly illustrated the power of words. "Divorce predictors" were everywhere. When the lady walked into the room, she couldn't look at me. She held her purse in front of her, close to her body. Whenever she talked, she looked at that purse rather than at the person to whom she was speaking. What made her behavior so fascinating to me was that it didn't align with her background. A few years before, this woman had been an officer in the military. She had led people and had won awards for leadership.

As I watched her interact with her husband over the three days of our workshop, I began to understand. He thought he was being helpful when he continually, repeatedly, and persistently corrected her. He would correct the way she pronounced words. When she would say she felt a particular emotion, he would say, “No, that's not really what you feel, you feel this instead.” Everything that he said to her—every word that he said—was in his mind communicating some good thought that would help her. That’s not what she was hearing. She heard relentless insults. She didn't feel liked or loved, and she absolutely did not feel respected. With an understanding of the dynamics of the marriage, we urged the husband to weigh his words carefully. We explained to him that his words were hurtful.

He responded, “Well, what I just said was true, and I didn't say it harshly, and I didn't say it spitefully. I’m being nice. My motivation is to help.”

We clarified that his personal motivation didn’t erase the damage he was doing to his wife. It was hurtful to her to feel continually criticized. We encouraged him that rather than trying to correct his wife, and rather than trying to be her father or her teacher, he should focus on being her husband.

Interestingly, by the third day of the workshop, this couple was completely changed. The husband finally understood the destructive nature of his criticism. At the same time, the wife was getting so much affirmation from the other people in the workshop that she began to revive that person she had been before—the confident leader. Other participants at the workshop were pointing out her positive characteristics and contributions. She heard people say, "I like the way you did that!" She began to believe in herself again because no one was constantly correcting her, chastising her, or putting her down.

If you want a healed and healthy spouse, make sure your words communicate your feelings of respect, even when you disagree. I believe very strongly in the power of words to heal or destroy. One time when I was sitting in an airport listening to a couple across the way, I even got up and intervened. I walked over to the man and asked, "Pardon me, sir, but is that your daughter?"

He was offended and became angry. "What do you mean is that my daughter? Why would you ask such a question?"

I replied, "Because you're treating her like a child."

Then I *ran* and got on my flight. My courage only goes so far.

Every word has power; every word you write and every word you say. So if you're thinking about calling a person a name, make sure it's a name like Darling, or Sweetheart, not a word that communicates condescension or disdain. When you use words wisely, everything changes.

Transparent, honest communication establishes an environment where intimacy and affection can flourish. In marriage, words of affirmation and honor enhance romance and affection.

There is a wonderful prayer in Proverbs where the wisest man who ever lived petitioned God: *May the words of my mouth and the meditations of my heart be wholly acceptable in Thy sight, Oh Lord, my strength and my redeemer.* He didn't just say, "Can my heart be good?" He asked, "Can you make my words good?"

The 9th Recipe

Think about how your spouse is hearing your words. Think past your motivation. Never justify what you say or how you say it by thinking your motivation is good. What really matters is how the other person hears the words, and how he or she reacts. Think not only in terms of your intent, but also in terms of the effect your words have on your spouse … intentional or not.

Don't always expect your spouse to agree with your point of view. When he or she doesn't, don't use the horsemen. Give respect. An expression such as, "That's not the way I see it, but I can see how you do," goes a long way.

Similarly, you can't require another person to have the emotional response you intend for them to feel. Even in painfully uncomfortable conversations, words of dignity and respect can create an environment of healing.

Chapter 10

The *Acceptance* Recipe

The greatest gift that you can give to others is the gift of unconditional acceptance and love.
—Brian Tracy

OFTEN I'M APPROACHED by a husband or wife with this question, "How can I change my spouse? I don't like what she's doing. I don't like what he is. What can I do to make him/her different?"

My answer is always the same. You can't do anything. There's nothing you can do to make another person be what you want them to be, or act like you want them to act. You could force some temporary changes because your spouse is afraid of some punishment or retaliation, but that's only going to last as long as the fear or threat lasts.

A husband and wife who had stalemated over this issue of change came for help. The husband wanted his wife to lose weight. In the course of the conversation she said, “Look, I know I'm overweight, and I'm happy to do something about it, but I will not lose weight to make him love me. When he can love me as I am, then I'll be glad to lose the weight.”

“Do you understand what she's saying?” I asked. “What she's saying is that you should change the way you're treating her. The only person you can control is you. The only actions you have control over are yours. Therefore, if you start loving her as she is, then she has the freedom to change.”

He said, “Wait a minute. Why should I do that?”

I repeated the famous Carl Rogers quote that I referenced earlier, “When I accept myself as I am, I change.” Then I continued with the rest of the quote. “When I accept others as they are, they change.”

As a general rule, people don’t like to change in order to win another person’s approval. People resist changing just because the other person demands it. That leads to resentment. In a marriage relationship, spouses want to be accepted and loved as they are, not threatened with the withdrawal of love if a change isn’t made. By contrast, when a spouse is accepted as he or she is, they have the freedom to change. The partner has the freedom then to become someone different, to become better at what she does, to lose the weight or whatever it might be because she already feels loved.

God demonstrated that kind of love for us. The book of Romans explains that while we were sinners Christ died for us. You may know of churches where people are told, "If you don't change, God's going to send you straight to hell." While theologically that might be correct, it's not the motivation that makes most people change. What gives us the ability to change? More likely, it's when people, empowered by the Holy Spirit, understand that God loves them and accepts His Son's sacrifice for their sin, so that they become favored and beloved. Valuing their acceptance by God, they begin to modify their behavior. They don't change so that God will love them; they change because He loves them.

Rather than looking at your spouse's actions and thinking, "Why can't you be what I want you to be or do what I want you to do?" look at yourself and consider "For every action there's a reaction." Newton's Laws of Motion happen both in relationships and in the scientific world. "If I can love you as you are, if I can be kind and gentle and sweet, if I can stop the behaviors that might be pushing you away, then that is what will give you the impetus to change. Therefore, any chance I have of changing you occurs only by my changing me. Then you may or may not change, it's still your choice. But now you won't resist changing because you feel loved as you are."

Allow me to speak from my personal experience. I have had many struggles with alcohol over the years. My concerned wife did an intervention with me several years ago to get me to go to Alcoholics Anonymous. The intervention was appropriate and necessary, but what really helped me to change was her demeanor. She never sat in judgment of me. In spite of my behavior, she continued to love me without reservation. She continued to be better and better at loving me. I reciprocated. I wanted to become what I'm supposed to be for her.

If you read what I just said as being a way to manipulate the other person to be everything you want them to be and do everything you want them to do, you missed my point. My point is to love the other person and accept him or her as he or she is. The change you make is in you. Interestingly, sometimes when you change you discover that things about the other person that bothered you before will not bother you at all. That may indicate that it wasn't the other person that needed to change, it was you.

The 10th Recipe

Quit trying to change other people. It will never work, and, besides that, if they change just because you want them to, they still won't be who you want. The recipe here is to accept the other person as he or she is, and then concentrate on yourself. Ask, "How can I be the best person I can possibly be? How can I be loving and kind and understanding and accepting? If I make the changes I need to, what will happen?" In all likelihood, the other person in your world will be drawn along and inspired to live better.

Chapter 11
The *Fair Fight* Recipe

Say what you mean, but don’t say it mean.
—Andrew Wachter

WHEN I WAS a kid I spent a night at a friend’s house. His family typically stayed up very late. At nearly one a.m., when I went running outside to play in the backyard, I let the door slam behind me. My friend’s dad heard the door slam and thought his wife had done it. I came back just in time to hear the argument start. It was intense. They were yelling at each other and calling each other names. I felt guilty and thought, “This is all my fault.”

As an adult, when I reflect on that scene I acknowledge that I set up the situation that instigated the fight, but the real cause was a problem in the relationship that was already there. This couple didn't know how to fight fair.

Every couple is going to have disagreements at some point. To all those couples who have been married fifty-plus years and claim, "My wife and I have never had an argument," let it be known that I'm doubtful. When I hear those claims, I instantly conclude that either they're lying or they're never home together. *Any* two people together enough will occasionally argue.

If you're going to fight fair, you have to establish the rules for fighting before the fight. Here are some suggested rules for fair fights.

1. We will keep it safe. Nobody is going to feel emotional or physical distress. Nobody is going to be afraid.

2. We will honor time outs. We're going to make a way to put on the brakes if things start getting out of hand. There can be a point when you get so angry that you really don't have much control over yourself any longer. Gottman calls this point 'flooding.' When emotional flooding occurs, adrenaline gets so high that the mind goes into a state where it fixates on detecting, identifying, preventing, avoiding, and stopping danger. Physiologically, the body begins to change: Blood begins to move away from the skin into the muscles. The body prepares to fight—I mean really fight—like they did back in the days of swords and shields. In a flooded state, people throw things

and punch walls. When a person gets that far, nothing good is going to happen.

You might be thinking, “My spouse and I would never do that.” I hope not, but one way to safeguard yourselves and your marriage is to include “time out” as one of the rules for fighting.

If an argument is not coming to a resolution, emotions are taking over, and a timeout should be called. All discussion should stop until everybody is calm. Start again *only* when each of you is calm and can maturely discuss matters. This is not only to prevent flooding, but to prevent anger-charged words from being spoken. We often say things we do not mean when we are angry. Though apologies may later be made for those words, cumulative damage can cause deep emotional wounds.

A time out can also be used if either of you starts yelling at the other. Do your very best to avoid yelling and shouting. It is difficult to empathize with someone who is yelling. Yelling at someone can do emotional damage in a similar way as words spoken in anger. Additionally, being yelled at can feel like the emotional equivalent of physical abuse.

Good ideas don’t require force. If you feel that you have to yell at your spouse to force him or her to do what you want or to see your point, perhaps you should rethink your approach.

The time out rule might include something like this: If a person calls time out, that person must bring up the subject again in a timely fashion. You can even set the timing in advance, such as "Whoever calls a time out must bring the subject up again within 24 hours." Another rule is that time out is only called because emotions are getting on edge. Using time out to avoid, stonewall, or manipulate is an abuse of the safeguard.

3. We will work together to resolve the problem. Damage is done when couples fight to hurt each other rather than focusing on resolving the problem.

A few years ago miscommunication with our crew led to my wife and I being the ones to set up one of our workshops. She and I were arranging the stage, the meeting rooms, and all the necessary equipment. Irritated that we had to do it ourselves when we had another appointment, Alice and I soon begin to growl at each other about how things were to be done. Soon we were in a full-blown argument. Then the irony of the situation hit me and I prayed aloud, "Oh, Lord, please don't let any couple come early. They'll walk in here and say, 'These are the people that are going to help us?!'" My wife started laughing and wisely suggested, "Let's call a time out. Let's back off from this, and when we get calm we'll set up the room." We sat and talked about something else for a few minutes and then finished the project. We weren't unhappy with each other, and the issue was resolved.

In the midst of a conflict, it can be helpful to picture you and your spouse sitting on opposite sides of the table. Then, mentally picture yourself getting up, going around to the other side of the table and sitting down on the same side as your partner. Now you're allies, both on the same side. You're not antagonists. Now you're trying to solve a problem; you're not trying to win or overcome the other person.

4. We will accept wise direction from a counselor or mentor. Rules 1-3 make arguments and resolutions sound easy and manageable. We all know that resolution can be very difficult, particularly when there's an emotional issue on the table. When the rules aren't working, you may benefit from a good mentor, counselor, minister, or a wise older couple that can help you as you discuss the problem. Decide beforehand who you will consult so that there is not a tendency to call on someone you believe is on "your side."

The 11th Recipe

Establish the rules for a fair fight at a time when you're not fighting. Suggested rules are:

1. We will keep it safe physically and emotionally.

2. We will honor time outs.

3. We will work together to resolve the problem, not win the argument.

4. We will accept counsel from a mentor we've agreed on.

If you work together to find a solution as opposed to fighting to hurt each other, reconciliation and resolution of conflict are possible.

Chapter 12
The *Healing Pain* Recipe

Where there is anger, there is always pain underneath.
—*Unknown*

A LADY FROM the east coast tracked me down by phone as I was speaking at Pepperdine University. Her husband was a minister who had been caught having an affair. When his church discovered the adultery, they terminated him. She left him and moved to another state to be with her parents. The discovery, dismissal, and separation all happened in a very short period of time.

After telling me the situation, she explained the purpose of her call. "My friends want me to do everything I can to punish him for what he has done. They are giving me all kinds of suggestions and advice on how to maximize his pain, and to make him pay for what he has done."

"How do you feel about that?" I inquired.

She wisely replied, "I have enough hurt of my own. I don't need to borrow any of theirs. Do you agree?"

I did.

She determined that she would not set out to punish him. She was hurt. He was hurt, as well. She saw no need to seek vengeance that would deepen the hurt for either of them. Her goal wasn't to intensify pain. She accepted it for what it was and was determined to heal. In her healing, she also found a blessing that likely would not have occurred if she had handled her pain as her friends wished her to. Eventually, they were reconciled and remarried.

Most of us have experienced pain somewhere in life. It can come into your life from any number of directions. It may have come from rejection or abuse when you were a child. The pain may have come from an unfaithful spouse who violated your trust. Maybe you experienced the pain of addiction in yourself or your spouse. I easily could write a hundred pages listing various sources of pain humans can experience.

Rather than discussing its origin, it would be better to discuss how to heal from it … and, even how to gain from it.

The recipe is to allow yourself to be human—at least to a certain extent—and then deal with pain in ways that moves you beyond it.

Many display their pain through anger. That's human, yet sometimes people don't recognize that their anger is pain manifesting itself. Actually, it's likely that any anger a person feels is based on hurt within. Whenever you ask someone why they are angry, they may respond, "I don't know." Want to know a better question to ask an angry person? Ask, "What hurts? Tell me about the hurt you feel." To heal and grow from pain rather than being captured by it, look for the pain underneath the anger. Understanding the pain is a strong first step to dealing with pain.

Be careful that as you deal with pain, you don't try to mask it.

Rather than confronting their pain, some try to cover it. Some do it with alcohol or other drugs, some become workaholics, some try for fame. This is another list that could take pages, but perhaps you get the idea. They attempt some type of self-medication by focusing on something or someone rather than going through the unpleasant and agonizing process of facing their pain and finding healing.

These people don't heal the pain; they dull it through their repetitive self-medication process. (You may have heard of it by another name—addiction. One can be addicted to a goal such as pursuing riches, to chemicals that alter the brain, or even to a person with whom one feels little to no pain while with them.)

There's an insightful life-understanding passage in Ephesians 4:19: "Having lost all sensitivity, they have given themselves over to sensuality so as to indulge in every kind of impurity." That phrase "having lost all sensitivity" could be translated as "feeling no pain." These people, rather than dealing with their pain, have masked it through a life of sensuality. I believe I have a good grasp on that verse because my life demonstrated it. Years ago I was in great pain because of things that had happened in my life. I dealt with the pain by drinking alcohol, mostly vodka, but would take anything I could get. The more alcohol I drank the less pain I felt. My attempts to dull pain were not unique. If you meet somebody who has been attending Alcoholic Anonymous meetings long enough to understand some things about themselves, you might ask "Why do you drink?" They likely will respond with words such as "I like the way it makes me feel." They don't necessarily mean the high that comes from drinking. They mean that as long as they are drinking, they don't feel pain.

Sadly, dulling the pain is not a substitute for dealing with it. Dealing with the pain may require consulting a professional. It may mean pouring the pain out before God alone.

The process can take a while. It can hurt. In the end, you'll probably discover that the pain will only be resolved through forgiveness. Whoever it is, whatever happened that caused you the pain, no matter your situation, usually peace after couple with every kind of pain you can possibly imagine follow steps of forgiveness and be reconciled. Often, as you would imagine, the hurt originates when one partner has been unfaithful to the other. Out of the pain, the betrayed spouse chooses to forgive not just the straying spouse, but also the affair partner. The betrayed spouse decides to view his or her mate and the paramour as flawed humans, even though emotions scream otherwise. After that decision, he or she decides not to take vengeance on either of them.

In our work with marriages affected by affairs, we find that most of the hurt spouses, who find the inner strength to do those first two steps, also take the step of reconciliation.

The 12th Recipe

If you wish to heal from your pain, even to grow something good out of the pain, understand your hurt. It's okay to be angry, but it's healthy to understand the pain beneath it.

Don't try to dull your pain through any type of self-medication. Face it, even if that means professional help. It may hurt, but hurting deeply for a short time is far better than hurting for years.

Ultimately, to heal you must accept whatever happened to hurt you. It is done. Accept that. Then move to forgiving all who hurt you, even if one of those people is you.

Forgiveness requires your deciding to view the other person as flawed rather than evil and choosing not to seek vengeance.

If you can—if it's safe emotionally, spiritually, physically—then learn to reconcile. If you don't know how, check my website at www.MarriageHelper.com for articles, eBooks, and podcasts that can help.

Chapter 13
The *Stop Controlling* Recipe

If God gave you a strong personality it's for
serving others, not controlling them.
—*Jimmy Evans*

THE MOST COMMON problem in troubled marriages that I work with is infidelity. The second most common problem is a controlling spouse.

Usually, the controlling spouse doesn't think of himself or herself as controlling. They try to control the way their mates act, think, and even feel, yet they seem oblivious to the fact that they are doing so. Yet, that doesn't counterbalance the negative effect their control has on the other.

"Not only does he regularly disagree with me on something I think, he continues to argue until finally I concede. I don't really agree; I just give up. He thinks his brilliant arguments convinced me. I'm thinking of different words than brilliant to describe him."

"I don't know why she doesn't get that I'm embarrassed when she corrects my grammar when I'm talking with people. When I later tell her how humiliated I was, she says her motive is to help and, therefore, I should quit being a baby and appreciate her help."

It can get much worse.

"He wants to know everyone I talk to, where I am every minute, and even tells me when I can see my parents."

"I'm afraid that if I don't do what she wants, the way she wants me to do it, she'll explode again. I walk on eggshells."

Admittedly, we witness more controlling husbands than wives. However, the following story about a domineering wife demonstrates the negative consequences of one spouse attempting to control another.

Some time ago, a couple came to our workshop. The wife was extremely domineering. She constantly told her husband what he should do. She tried to control everything that occurred in their lives. The husband was not weak, but he was more laid back than she. She was the one who would say, "Do it this way. Do it now. NO! Do it right." They came to our workshop because she had been involved with another man, yet she felt entitled to demand forgiveness from her husband, seemingly ignoring his pain and need for healing. She even set out the terms of his forgiveness for her. She dominated and controlled the relationship.

It seemed that some progress had been made during the workshop. One morning, they went for a walk together. As they walked, she got a cramp and wanted to return to the hotel room. He stated, “I'll go with you.”

To which she replied, “No, you need to walk. You walk the rest of the way.”

He answered, “But you don't understand, I'm only here to spend time with you. We're doing this workshop together. I want to be with you.”

She persisted, “No, you must walk. It's another mile. You go on. I'll go back to the hotel alone.”

Whether to walk or return to the hotel seems like a minor thing. It wasn’t. That command became the final feather that made the weight too much to bear. He decided “That's it, I'm done.”

That marriage could have been saved. It was actually on track and I had felt very good about their progress during our workshop. All she had to do was stop controlling. To treat him as an equal who could make his own choices in life. To no longer act as his parent, but as his partner.

Controlling eventually destroys relationships. The marriage may not end in divorce, but the relationship—the equal exchange of ideas, respect, trust, and warmth—dies.

When one person in a marriage attempts to control the other, the marriage deteriorates. No matter what your motive, never become the 'parent' who tells the other what to think, do, or feel. The secret is to have an egalitarian marriage—each of you is equal and should be treated that way.

The 13th Recipe

If you are controlling, stop. Even if it makes you nervous, even if you, as of yet, know no other way to operate, even if you feel you are the wisest, smartest, or strongest. If your spouse views you as a dictator, he or she very likely is losing love for you month by month, year by year.

If you are the spouse feeling controlled, stand up for yourself. Do not allow your spouse to treat you as an inferior. If you can't stand up for yourself because you fear your spouse, seek help to overcome your abuse.

Chapter 14
The *Conflict Defining* Recipe

The most important thing in communication is
hearing what isn't said.
—Peter Drucker

A COUPLE WHO came to our Marriage Helper 911 Workshop had been in conflict for months. They thought they were fighting about one thing when they actually were fighting over something else altogether. The wife wanted to start working outside the home. She had been staying home to raise their child. Now the child was going to the first grade, and she wanted to get a job. The husband was adamant: "My wife will not work outside the home." (That may sound like an antiquated problem, but for this couple, the debate was real.)

We helped them understand that the work-outside-the-home question was a symptom of something deeper. They needed to get to the root of their problems. I began by asking him questions like “What do you think about when you think about your wife working outside the home?”

The questions led him back to his own childhood. He said, “I was a latchkey kid before the phrase ‘latchkey kid’ was coined. My father worked, and my mother worked. Every bit of trouble I ever got into in my life happened when I was at home and finding nobody there.”

I asked the wife, “What does it mean to you to work outside the home?”

She spoke of her childhood, “I'm an only child. My mother was a very successful business woman. She made her mark on the world, and I want to do the same. I want to feel that I'm doing something in addition to being a mother and a homemaker.”

I pointed out to him, “Do you understand that you're not fighting over whether or not she works outside the home? What you're fighting over is whether or not you feel that your son is going to have the care he needs while your wife is working outside the home. The only way you know to ensure your son’s safety is to have your wife at home with him. If you two can find a way for her to work outside the home, which provides a way for one of you to be home when your son gets home, your problem would be solved.”

When an opening came available for a position as teacher’s assistant at their child’s school, they agreed that this position met each of their desires. Both husband and wife were happy, but they never would have solved the problem had they not understood the underlying issues.

Many of the things that people fight about are not what they think they're fighting about at all.

The 14th Recipe

When you find yourself in perpetual conflict over the same issue and unable to find a resolution, ask yourselves questions such as these:

> "What does this mean to me?"
>
> "What conviction am I fighting for?"

And more like those.

Understand how each person understands the situation. Identify what it is that each person values enough to fight for. That's how you find the root of persistent problems.

When you've identified the real issue, you can harmonize and work out a solution.

Chapter 15

The *Shared Goals* Recipe

Many marriages would be better if the husband and the wife clearly understood that they are on the same side.

—Zig Ziglar

IN OUR EARLY years of marriage, I was on the road quite a bit for speaking engagements while Alice was home with our children. My speaking around the country and Alice's caregiving for our kids actually pulled us in different directions because we were pursuing different life goals.

It's okay for each spouse to have his or her own goals, but with too many marriages there is no shared goal. When that happens, nearly every couple inevitably drifts apart.

When a couple finds a common goal, a common dream, a shared vision to pursue together that fulfills each of them, they reach levels of intimacy most couples will never know exist. That doesn't mean each gives up his or her individuality. It doesn't mean that one quits doing those things that are important to that person. It does mean they put as much or more energy into their joint plans as they do into their individual plans.

I vividly remember how this worked in the life of one couple. On Friday morning of our workshop the husband announced, “This marriage is over. I'm just here because I feel like I should give it one last shot, but there is no hope for us.” On Sunday, our third day of workshop, he walked back into the workshop, saying, “We just bought a popup camper on eBay. It's going in the bed of our pickup truck.”

Somewhat surprised, one of our team members asked him to continue.

He said, “We got to talking over the weekend and realized that she used to go camping when she was a child, and that was how her family created great times together. I went camping when I was a child, too. Camping was when my family got together. We realized that we could camp with our children and have this tremendous thing where we all spend time together and enjoy each other. It’s a common interest that we both enjoy.”

Buying a camper on eBay doesn't sound profound, but in actuality it was. It changed the direction of their marriage.

Their commonality—their common goal—became "We will come together as a family and do something that we enjoy. We like camping." They didn't let their limited budget stop their dreams. They agreed on a camper on the back of the pickup.

Alice and I also changed direction toward a common goal. We realized we were drifting apart. Together we started considering what we could pursue together, which would utilize both of our gifts and talents. We decided that we'd start doing workshops dedicated to helping marriages in crisis. We'd been in crisis early in our lives—a crisis so serious we had divorced and remarried. Our new vision turned us toward each other. I continued to travel to speak, but not as much. Alice continued to be a wonderful homemaker. Yet, it was different. Our common goal drew us together. Every month we did a workshop for marriages in crisis, and Alice and I were right there together, both using our gifts, both fulfilled, both going the same direction. It has brought us closer than anything we'd ever done in our lives.

The 15th Recipe

Find your common goal. Discuss things such as:

> What would we like to fulfill that we haven't done?
>
> What did we say we are going to do when we were young that we haven't yet completed?

> What gifts do each of us have that we can put together to accomplish something significant?
>
> What need exists that really touches the hearts of both of us?

Find a common purpose that uses the gifts of both partners and brings worth to the world around you.

Chapter 16
The *Honest to God* Recipe

Honesty before God requires the most fundamental risk of faith we can take: the risk that God is good, that God does love us unconditionally. It is in taking this risk that we rediscover our dignity. To bring the truth of ourselves, just as we are, to God, just as God is, is the most dignified thing we can do in this life.
—*Gerald May*

I REMEMBER AS a child I'd go to church dressed in clothes I never wore any other day. I always got a lecture from my mom before we arrived, "Now, don't you act like you normally act. Behave yourself at church!"

Church was a ritual that had nothing to do with my every-day life. On Sunday we went to a place I otherwise avoided, wearing clothes I never wore, and acting like I never acted. In other words, on Sunday mornings I wasn't 'me' at all. Though my mother never intended it, our weekly façade gave me the impression that God wasn't happy with the real me, and I had better pretend to be somebody else if I wanted God to like me.

Unfortunately, over the years I began to understand that a lot of people try to approach God wearing whatever metaphorical fig leaves they could find to hide their true selves from Him.

We pretend that our shroud is adequate to cover our shame. We pretend to be holy. We pretend to be better than we are. We'll do anything to avoid exposing our real selves.

In the first chapter of this book, we addressed the challenges to intimacy with a spouse. Unfortunately, our attempts to find acceptance extend to our relationship with God. We're afraid to be ourselves before an omnipotent, omniscient God.

If we really want to grow closer to God, the only way is follow that old hymn of our grandparents, "Just as I Am."

Our sins indicate that while we believe in one sense that God sees and knows everything, we also believe in another sense that he doesn't. After all, if we truly believed He sees everything, there are some things we've done that we wouldn't have. (Can I get an amen?!)

How do we get our theology and our life to align? The answer is to use the same method that we use to create intimacy with another person. We start taking off the bricks to reveal ourselves to the God who sees and knows all. Yes, it works even if we believe He already knows. This is an act we willfully do to open ourselves to him.

We start talking to God.

When you're tempted by something, without using some kind of holy church language, but in language you would normally use, tell God, “I'm tempted by this particular situation.” If you feel anger towards somebody, tell God about that. Talk it over with Him. Tell God about your joys. Tell God about your sorrows. Tell Him about your aspirations. Tell Him about your disappointments. Become transparent and honest and open to God completely.

No, I haven't reached the pinnacle of that myself, but over the years, I have become more transparent with God. I can be honest enough with Him in my prayer life to say, “This particular thing happened today, and it tempted me. Lord, I want to talk with you about it for a while.” It has changed the way I pray. It has also changed the way I perceive God because it changes the way that I view God's view of me.

Many of us think we've got to be somebody else for God to love us, but Romans 5:6-8 reveals that God loves us as we are, even while we are sinners. I don't have to meet any artificial standard set by any person, no matter whom that person might be, for God to love me. He sees me flawed. Romans 3:23 tells me “For everyone has sinned; we all fall short of God's glorious standard." Yet, He loves me anyway.

Before God, I accept and admit that that's who I am—unrighteous, sinful, and weak. I know God loves me anyway. He loves me with my imperfections. He loves me with my flaws, my struggles, and my sins. That realization develops a deeper relationship with God because now it's intimate.

Remember, we said earlier that intimacy is sometimes defined as "into me see." I let God see into me by telling Him the deceitfulness of my heart. Yes, He knows that already, but by talking to Him about it, by being honest and transparent about it, now I internalize that He sees me and loves me 'just as I am.'"

Transparency before God opens the way for intimacy in marriage. If you pray aloud with your spouse, transparent prayer also brings you closer to each other. Transparency with God in front of a spouse allows you to bear each other's burdens, grieve together, encourage each other, and honor each other.

The 16th Recipe

Pray transparently to develop a deeper intimacy with God. Discuss everything with Him, including the not-so-good things you feel, say, or do. Allow yourself to bask in His love by accepting that you don't have to be perfect; He loves you just as you are.

People who can pray together out loud, transparently, about their own flaws, their own weaknesses, their own temptations, find closeness to God and closeness to their spouse. Understanding that God loves me like I am, flawed and all, gives me the ability to believe that my spouse can also love me 'just as I am.'

Chapter 17
The *Real Jesus* Recipe

Jesus lived a life that was full of joy and contradictions and fights, you know? If they were to paint a picture of Jesus without contradictions, the gospels would be fake, but the contradictions are a sign of authenticity.
—*Paulo Coehlo*

I WAS TALKING to a Nazarene pastor friend, Dwight Gunter of Trevecca Community Church, about people who don't share our Christian faith. He told me an interesting story about a conversation with a person who said, "I don't believe in Jesus."

"Tell me what you know about Jesus," encouraged Dwight.

The non-believer talked for a while and then concluded by saying, "That is my understanding of who Jesus is."

Dwight responded, “I don't believe in that Jesus either. Let me tell you about the real Jesus, not the one that you heard about on television or that you think exists. Let me share with you who God really is, and then maybe you'll have a different view of God altogether.”

If you think that only non-Christians and the unchurched are impacted by a faulty view of God, and that all Christians have the right view of God and of Jesus, please reconsider. As I talk to people about their spiritual lives and relationships, I hear a variety of different views and concepts that many Bible-believing Christians have of God.

Some think that God is vindictive, waiting for us to do something wrong so He can cast us into hell. Others have a picture of God as a benevolent father who doesn't really care what we do as long as we generally wind up on the right side of things. Of course, there are many views that fall between those extremes.

How can we know who God is?

God has spoken to us in His scriptures, and if you really want to understand God, I suggest that you start reading the bible again—the whole thing starting with Genesis. However, this time, do it a little differently. After you read each story, stop and put yourself in the place of the various characters in that Bible story. If you are Abraham or Joseph or Esther from the Old Testament, or perhaps Peter or Paul or Joanna from the New Testament, consider, “How would I have reacted if that had been me?”

When I taught Bible at a Christian university, I assigned all my students a role in the story found in Luke 7 where Jesus stopped a funeral procession and raised a widow's son. Some students were to play the role of the widow burying her only son, some were apostles, others the funeral crow, and I assigned one to be the dead son. I told all of them to read the story before they came back to class and to consider how they themselves would have reacted if they had been there. I wanted them to get a deeper understanding of who Jesus is based on how they would react to what He did that day.

I asked the young woman I had assigned to play the role of the mother, "So this complete stranger tells your dead son to get up, how would you react at that point?"

She said, "How dare he interfere! I don't know who this man is. Why is he breaking my heart?"

I said. "And how would you react when the boy sat up and began to talk?"

"I'd be full of joy."

"And how would this event change your understanding of Jesus?"

I followed the same process with every student who had been assigned a role from that story.

Why?

I wanted them to put themselves in Bible stories. Not to discount the real story, I wanted them to grasp that. However, I wanted them to internalize the story, what it meant, and what it tells us about God.

I think if you use a similar process, you can get a deeper understanding of who God is, not as you wish Him to be, but as His interaction with people reveals Him to be.

Let me give you an example of what Bible stories teach us about humanity and God's interaction with us.

John the Baptist was thrown into prison. Prior to his imprisonment, he had proclaimed that Jesus was the Son of God. Yet, when Jesus didn't come to get him out of prison, he sent his disciples to ask Jesus if He *really* was the Messiah, the Son of God. He doubted that Jesus was the Messiah because Jesus didn't do what he expected Him to do. A lot of people have experienced doubts like John the Baptist. They pray, "God, give me this. God, do this for me." When God doesn't do what they expect, they begin to doubt that God is there.

Once a minister recounted to me that he had prayed and felt that God had led him to a particular church. Things hadn't gone well. He was left questioning, "Why would God do that to me? Maybe God is not really there."

My first thought was to remind him, "You prayed. God answered. He sent you there. Obviously God used you for good. Can you really judge God's nature based on the fact that it didn't turn out the way you wished it to?" Instead, I read the story of John's questioning whether Jesus was really the Messiah. I asked him why he thought John felt that way. But, before he answered, I told him it would be good to imagine himself as John in that dungeon. If he were John in that situation, what would he be thinking? Feeling?

The proverbial light bulb came on.

"If I were John, I think I'd be feeling just what I'm feeling now."

Then we read the rest of the story together and Jesus's gentle answer to John's doubts. I said, "Maybe that's similar to what He's saying to you now."

My friend got the message. Not just in his head, but in his heart.

If we believe God is sovereign, we understand that God does what is best, and we accept Him as He is. Then we love the true God, not the God we create in our minds.

The 17th Recipe

Get to know the God of the Bible. One way to do that is to insert yourself into Bible stories to try to understand the story emotionally, not just intellectually, so that it touches not just your mind, but your heart and your soul.

When you do that, you may well develop a healthier concept of God.

How does that apply to marriage?

Difficulties occur in most marriages. In hard times, one or both of you may question God and His character. If you begin to place yourself in the Bible, you'll see God as He really is. Don't start with a preconceived notion, but let God reveal himself to you in His word. You can know His anger at sin and His compassion for those in pain. You can hear His voice. A proper concept of God and His sovereignty strengthens your relationship to both God and your spouse.

Chapter 18
The *Great Sex* Recipe

Sex is God's wedding gift to you.
—*Unknown*

FOR SEVERAL YEARS I've taught human sexuality at a Christian university. Every semester, I have students come into the class wondering how we will address the subject of human sexuality in a Christian environment. Some find themselves shocked in the very first class when they realize that we'll discuss sex very openly and honestly. I tell them that sex was invented by God. He's actually in favor of it! It creates a wonderful experience of bonding between two human beings.

In most of nature, sex is designed to create offspring. It's more than that with humans. When it comes to the relationship between a loving husband and wife, sex, in addition to procreating babies, also creates a bond of the heart, of the mind, of the soul, and of the body. That kind of relationship in the bedroom is what God wants us to have.

During my online live call-in radio program, a caller shared her disappointment with the way she had been taught about sex. “I'm a Christian. I'm thirty-five years old, and I've been taught all of my life ‘Sex is wrong. Sex is wrong. Sex is wrong.’ The day before I got married, I was told, ‘Sex is good.’ I know God made sex for marriage, but in my conscience, I can't make the transition. I've been married fifteen years and still any time I enjoy a sexual experience with my husband, I feel guilty. I wish some Christian leader would tell me it's okay to enjoy sex with my husband.”

Some will have read the previous paragraph and thought, “That’s an anomaly. Most Christians aren’t subjected to teaching about sex that keeps them from enjoying it in marriage.” Others read it with sadness because that’s exactly what happened to them.

We Christians need to teach that sex, in the right context, is wonderful.

When our daughter Joanna was about to reach puberty, my wife came to me and said, “Because you’re a sexologist, Joe, I want you to tell Joanna about the birds and the bees.”

I replied, “She's the daughter and you're the mama, so you tell her.”

Alice said, “I want you to do it.”

"You're the mama," I said.

"I want you to do it."

"You're the mama!"

Alice outlasted me on that argument. So I sat down with Joanna and began to talk to my daughter about sex. Alice was there to make sure that I'd got everything correct. I told my daughter about the anatomical parts and how they work; and then I said to her, "But what you need to understand is that sex will be the most wonderful way you can say to your husband 'I love you,' and the most wonderful way he can say to you, 'I love you.' As you get older, you'll be dating some boy, and he might kiss you. You'll begin to feel hormones surge through your body. When that happens, just think to yourself, 'Thank you, God, for the preview of coming attractions,' and then you tell the boy to bring you home. The sexual bond is so unique that you should have it only with your husband. It'll be the most unique and wonderful relationship you can have with him."

I wanted my daughters to know that the sexual union in marriage is a wonderful, beautiful relationship between two people.

I could address all kinds of things about sex, but because of space limitations I must consider only the most basic principles.

For example, often I'm asked, "What are the boundaries? What are those things we can't do?" (I was even asked that question by Lester Holt on the Today Show. He may not ask that frank of a question on live, unedited TV again.)

I could give you a list of the various passages in the Old Testament that tell you things you can't do like commit adultery or incest. But, instead I will sum up all of the Biblical rules in a few sentences.

Sex is to be only with your spouse and no one else—both in reality and in fantasy. You may recall that Jesus said that if a man lusts after another woman, he has committed adultery in his heart. Pornography includes someone who is not a spouse, so it is to be avoided.

Not only can sex not involve any person other than your spouse, sex can't involve any animal.

Finally, sex can't create harm or cause harm to either of you--mentally, emotionally, spiritually, or physically.

I believe that all the teachings about sex in the Bible are summed up in the above principles. Because those are the only prohibitions, there is a tremendous variety that can happen in the bedroom, which a Christian couple can use to fulfill each other.

In addition to my university students, I often speak to groups of Christian husbands and wives about sex. They ask a lot of questions about sex, though seldom verbally; they prefer to anonymously write their questions. The consistent theme of the questions is an interest and pursuit in how to enjoy each other to the greatest degree. Whether

I'm addressing couples or university students who are anticipating marriage, my message is the same: "Within marriage, enjoy each other. Don't do anything that causes either one of you harm, mentally, emotionally, spiritually, physically. Enjoy each other in every other way you possibly can. Have fun with each other and focus on fulfilling each other in every way, and that will give you the life that you want. And if you find that you have some inhibitions, the best way to get past those inhibitions is to learn how to pray together transparently. If you are both on your knees, addressing God, talking about your own struggles, your own temptations aloud next to each other, it will cause the transparency you have with God to also become part of the transparency you have with each other. It's amazing how many inhibitions go away when you pray together. So, yes, prayer can make sex better."

Interestingly, secular researchers have studied the difference between good sex and great sex. Their findings indicate that it comes down to focusing on your spouse. As a matter of fact, the research is very compatible with the scriptural command to submit to the other person. Submitting leads to trusting each other, allowing one to be totally in the moment, immersed in the pleasure that is given.

The 18th Recipe

Enjoy sex. God intended for you to. Enjoy being completely open and transparent with each other in sex. Enjoy revealing all of yourself to someone who is going to touch, kiss, and love all of you as you are. Make it your goal to fulfill your spouse and you will have a sex life that will be fulfilling as long as you live.

Chapter 19

The *Smart Boundaries* Recipe

Protect your marriage: keep boundaries with the opposite sex.
—*IntentionalToday.com*

WHEN WE WORK with couples in crisis, we witness a high percentage of marriages that have been shaken by infidelity. Most of the time, the one who was unfaithful never intended to stray. Good people don't typically plan things such as "I think I'll go have an affair," or "I think I'll leave my spouse for somebody else." Usually, unfaithful spouses are good people who allowed themselves to get into situations where they crossed boundaries. They neglected to put up safeguards at the outset because they thought, "We're just friends. Nothing bad is going to happen."

Characteristically, an affair happens when a man and woman start talking to each other to the point that they take bricks off their walls. They reveal themselves as they really are, becoming transparent and open with the other person. The friendship grows deeper and deeper. By the time they realize they're about to cross the boundary into an affair, they don't stop because the relationship feels too good.

After crossing smaller boundaries, the initial guilt begins to subside, and they start to believe, "This person understands me like no one else ever has. We're as close to each other as we can possibly be. My spouse doesn't understand or love me like this." I've even heard people deeply involved emotionally with a lover say, "I'm married, but I'm sure that God sent my lover to me because we're just so compatible."

How can a person ensure that he or she is never unfaithful? How can couples help each other to never fall into those situations?

Set smart and reasonable boundaries.

In our marriage, Alice and I agreed that she would monitor any interaction I have with women. For example, if somebody wants to meet with me and Alice says "I'm not comfortable with that," I don't do it. You might be thinking "You're being controlled by your spouse." No, not at all; I offered her that part of my life.

I asked her to use her radar to protect me. I might not realize (or may not be willing to admit) that I'm attracted to a person, but Alice knows me well and can protect me from my own naïveté. It's not only whether I might be attracted to the woman. I may not realize that the other person is attracted to me, but Alice has a perceptive read on that.

Why do we do that? I deal with unfaithful men and women regularly. They get into those situations because they don't acknowledge the dangers of being open and transparent with people other than their spouses.

Does that mean you can't have a friend you can be open and transparent with? No. You can have that kind of friend. But make sure it's a friend of your same gender. Make sure it's somebody that you can't possibly develop an inappropriate relationship with.

One well known business that I speak for occasionally has a rule that states: One man and one woman can never be alone in a room together, at any time, unless they're married to each other. If it's just the two of them, one of them has to leave. You may say, "Well, that sounds awfully rough. I mean, are you saying they don't trust anybody?" That's not the point at all. They, like I, have seen so many unwitting coworkers, friends, or community members become intimate after normal, innocent conversations gradually became too open and transparent. What's the best way to keep that from happening? It's not to stop it while it's in progress; it's to put up boundaries, which protect both married and non-married people.

The 19th Recipe

Adhere to the boundaries that protect you and your marriage. All too often, the people that get into trouble by crossing boundaries with another person never intended to. Usually, they are good people who failed to establish the right boundaries and fell into crisis.

Together, as husband and wife, establish boundaries and then give each other permission to enforce the boundaries.

What boundaries should be put in place? Have friends, but don't have a friend of the opposite gender that you spend time with alone.

When you want to reveal your secrets in life; when you're ready to laugh and dream; go to your spouse.

Chapter 20
The *Hope* Recipe

Motto for the bride and groom: we are a work in progress with a lifetime contract.
—*Phyllis Koss*

I MET A couple in their seventies who had been married for over 50 years and were still so much in love that when one of them left the room, the other person missed his/her mate. When the spouse who had left the room-just to go to the kitchen to get a glass of water-returned, the other one would beam, "I am so glad you are back." Their love was strong and evident.

I am sure that their marriage had not been perfect because no marriage ever is, but they made it through a lifetime together. They learned how to solve their problems and how to stay in love.

If your marriage is like that, congratulations. Thank you for staying in it. Thank you for not quitting even when things got tough.

Unfortunately, at-risk marriages are abundant.

A few years ago a friend was telling me about his friends. He said, "Nobody in this county believes that they can make it. The husband is madly in love with the other woman." Previously, this straying husband had lived a good Christian life, but by that point, he had taken on a different personality. His wife was praying for restoration. Everyone who knew them predicted doom and destruction for their marriage.

By the grace and power of God, and the urging of people who knew them well, a friend of theirs got the couple to enroll in one of my workshops for marriages in crisis. Afterwards, I met with the husband several times, individually for coffee, over the next few weeks. He went from "I am so much in love with this other person; I never want to go back to my wife; my wife is terrible" to "My wife is ever faithful; I've brought great pain to the one whom I love; I will do all I can to work toward restoring our marriage."

Over the weeks we met, the wife continued to be loving. She continued to be compassionate. She didn't become vindictive or angry. She continued to pray every day for their marriage. Through her efforts and through God working on this man's heart, they put their marriage back together. They are still married to this day. Even better, they now help other couples who are in trouble. They have helped save many other marriages.

Why?

Because she wouldn't quit. She stayed right in there and did the things she should do. Many people were telling her, "Let it go. Divorce him. Move on." She refused to let go until she knew that there would be no hope for the marriage. For them, that point of no hope was avoided.

Another couple we worked with told a story about how she had come home one night and told him that she was no longer in love with him, that she wasn't about to stay in this marriage anymore, and that life would be much better if she were on her own instead of with him.

After delivering that message, she went to bed and fell into a deep sleep because what she had said was so emotional and she was exhausted.

Her husband did something fascinating. He sat next to her bed all night long, praying. He prayed for her, he prayed for her heart, he prayed for what had happened in their relationship. He prayed for all those things, and all night long never left her side and never quit praying. She slept the night without once waking. His prayers were silent; no audible sound broke the quiet.

When she woke up the next morning, she turned and looked at him. He was still beside her praying. She said, "Something changed. I don't know what happened, but it has. I don't want to leave you anymore. In my heart, I want to love you. I want to make this marriage work." And they did.

That husband still prays today.

Even though they are very much in love and very much together today, there are still nights when he prays over her and their marriage through the silent hours as she sleeps.

If you keep doing the right thing there is always a hope that your marriage can be salvaged, and beyond being salvaged, made good. When we work with marriages in trouble, our goal is never just to keep spouses together, although, in the short term, there can be great value in keeping them together. Our goal is always to help couples solve their problems. Then we help guide them through learning how to be in love with each other again. We want couples to see a great future ahead.

I can assure you from my own experience, the marriage that Alice and I have now is so much better than the one that we had before we divorced in the 1980s. If we were the only couple that could make that statement, it would be an anomaly. We've worked with scores of couples over the last twenty years who will tell you, "We are happier now, after overcoming our problems, than we ever were before."

There is tremendous value in not quitting.

There's value in saving your so-so marriage so you can grow into a wonderful marriage.

The 20th Recipe

Through rough times that come to your marriage, always have hope in God, and continue to stand for your marriage as long as you can.

Pray with all of your heart.

Continue to do the things that you need to do.

Be comforted to know that even in situations where everybody else gives up hope and says that it can't work, it can. But only if you don’t quit. That's the secret. No matter how tough things become, no matter how difficult life can be, *don't quit.*

Chapter 21

The *Mutual Acceptance* Recipe

Love is friendship that has caught fire. It is quiet understanding, mutual confidence, sharing and forgiving. It is loyalty through good and bad times. It settles for less than perfection and makes allowances for human weaknesses.

—Ann Landers

FALLING IN LOVE often follows a familiar course. First two people find themselves attracted to each other.

They may be attracted physically. "You're hot!"

They may be attracted intellectually. "We really have a lot of common interests and we understand each other."

They may be attracted emotionally. "The things that you do evoke emotions within me that I really enjoy feeling."

They may be attracted spiritually. "I really admire the way you think. I like the morals and beliefs and the values you have."

If it's physical, intellectual, emotional, spiritual, or any combination thereof, attraction draws us closer to that other person. However, attraction and closeness don't constitute love. It can constitute a very strong attraction, which sometimes people feel is love and sometimes refer to as love at first sight. But the love that keeps a couple together comes after the initial attraction.

Love is when they learn to accept each other.

You see, you can't love anybody you don't accept, not even yourself. In this book we've talked about the connection between loving another person and accepting yourself (learning to love yourself as you are.)

That doesn't mean you always love the things you do because we're all imperfect. We wind up thinking things and doing things that we don't feel good about, but you learn to accept yourself even though you're flawed. God loves you and He knows everything about you. You can love yourself, as well. And when you do accept yourself as you are, you change because you have the liberty and ability to change.

When you accept yourself as you are, you have the basis for developing a real true love relationship with another person. It provides you with the ability to learn how to accept the other person as he or she is. You allow that person to take bricks off their wall and become transparent. You won't always like what they think, you won't always like what they feel, and you won't always like what they have done or even what they're doing. Nevertheless, when you can learn to accept the other person, even when he/she doesn’t live up to your original expectations, you can develop this true, honest love.

Acceptance leads to a desire to communicate with each other because now you're not just trying to make your own point while the other person hears what you think. You're also genuinely and honestly listening in an effort to understand the other person’s thoughts and emotions. You want to know what is in the heart and mind of your lover.

When misunderstandings occur, you get past them by seeking out the values you both hold dear. You discern if what you're arguing about is really what you’re arguing about. You attempt to understand your spouse’s thoughts, reactions, and emotions.

As you engage in communication about heart matters and endeavor to understand your spouse, you come to share a life together. You share your dreams. You find that ambition that you can pursue together, which uses each of your gift sets. It becomes a mutual purpose and aspiration that is uniquely yours because it uses your individual gifts to achieve a common ambition. This common goal pulls you together when life works to pull you apart.

You also come together to enjoy the bedroom. Because we are physical beings as well as spiritual beings, we communicate married love to another person by making love—uninhibited, open, transparent love. To do that, you must understand that what happens inside the bedroom is affected by everything that happens outside the bedroom. And so, you develop the trust, the understanding, the compassion, the ability to count on the other person, the commitment to know the other person will be there no matter what. Equally, everything that happens inside the bedroom affects what happens outside the bedroom. And so, that loving, openness, transparency, commitment, lack of inhibition, and total surrender to each other in the bedroom benefits all those things that happen outside the bedroom.

Marriage changes as you get older. Your body changes physically. Your experiences in life clarify your perspective. You become more mature. You won't see the world the same at forty as you did at twenty; your outlook will likely adjust again by the time you're sixty.

But as you mature and develop together, hand in hand, working through life, it's a continual courtship—always caring about the other person, always being there for him or her. And by the time you reach the later years of life, you can celebrate that you didn't quit. Despite any encountered struggles and heartache, you didn't quit. You did what it took to resolve the problems; you overcame.

And finally, when you get to the end of this life, you are still married to each other, hand in hand, loving and hoping.

You grieve the anguish that death's separation brings and long for the reunion in heaven. That's the kind of marriage that you can have when you start today to embrace the marriage recipes in this book.

About the Author

Dr. Joe Beam is an internationally-known inspirational speaker and best-selling author. He founded Marriage Helper, INC, and serves as its chairman. He has spoken to millions of people worldwide in personal appearances as well as appearances on television and radio, including *ABC's Good Morning America, Focus on the Family, the Montel Williams Show, NBC's Today Show, The Dave Ramsey Show, The Morning Show with Mike and Juliet* and magazines such as *People* and *Better Homes and Gardens.*

Joe holds the Ph.D in Biomedical science at the University of Sydney, with an emphasis on sexology. Joe earned his bachelor's degree (Magna Cum Laude) at Southern Christian University, and did graduate studies in Clinical Psychology at the University of Evansville.

Connect With Dr. Joe Beam

If your marriage is in trouble,
http://www.joebeam.com/troubled_marriages.htm

To order books written by Joe Beam,
http://www.joebeam.com/books.htm

To schedule Joe for a presentation to your church or organization, http://www.joebeam.com/seminar_info.htm

To read articles written by Joe Beam,
http://www.joebeam.com/articlesbyjoe.htm

See Joe's blog on sex for expert suggestions.
http://www.joebeam.com/sex_blog

Become a Facebook fan of Joe's book, *Seeing the Unseen*
https://www.facebook.com/SeeingTheUnseen/?fref=ts

Become a Facebook fan of Joe's book, *The True Heaven*
https://www.facebook.com/TheTrueHeaven/

Also see Joe Beam's Google Profile Page
https://plus.google.com/+JoeBeamphd/posts